Wildlife *in* Words

A collection of poetry
by
Otley Writers & Otley Stanza

Copyright © The copyright remains with the individual authors 2024

The right to be identified as authors of these works has been asserted by them in accordance with the Copyright, Designs and Patents Act 1988.

All rights reserved. No part of this publication may be reproduced, stored in a retrieval system, or transmitted in any form or by means, electronic, mechanical, photocopying, recording, or otherwise, without the prior permission of the author.

A CIP catalogue record for this title is available from the British Library.

ISBN 9798342638258

Foreword

This collection of poetry is a collaboration between Otley Writers and Otley Stanza. Both groups meet in the Courthouse Arts and Resource Centre.

It has been published as part of the Otley Wildlife Arts Festival 2024.

Otley Writers & Otley Stanza

OTLEY WRITERS

Otley Writers are a creative writing group of authors who produce work in a wide range of disciplines and a diverse range of genres.

A strong legacy of poetry was created by the renowned poet James Nash who led the group before his retirement in 2017. The current members follow in the footsteps of Christine Moran and the late Glenda Kerney Brown

John Ellis

John is the writer J.R. Ellis, author of the bestselling Yorkshire Murder Mystery novels. These are set in the varied landscapes and communities of the county he loves and where he has lived most of his life. He began writing after retiring from a career in teaching, mostly in further education. As well as crime novels John writes poetry and short stories.
He is the mentor of Otley Writers.

Otley Writers & Otley Stanza

Nature's Play

The woods have a glorious
New spring perfection,
Of colour, shape and sound.
I ache to press time's shutter,
And keep this fresh green beauty forever.
But time never stops,
And change is certain.
Each year nature performs
A play in several acts,
Each growing from the last.
Without autumn colours,
And white winter snows,
The green of May
Would lose its meaning.
Transience forces attention.
Look, Now. Listen, Now.
I notice the seeding cow parsley,
The darkening leaves,
The fading dawn chorus,
And welcome the next act.

Ash Die Back

This spring there is death in the woods
Amongst the new life.
Trees are unfurling bright leaves
In beautiful canopies.
But the ash falters.
Green on some branches,
Winter bareness still on others.
Around us spindly corpses,
Trees which have lost the fight
Against disease.
The ash has a simple message:
Nature itself is struggling.
It could shed its leaves and die,
And nothing will bring it back.

Spring Hibernation
Written during the Covid lockdown

As the sun grows warmer,
We shrink into shadows.
The lark soars,
But we hunker down.
While flowers bloom,
Our lives turn grey.

Nature's rebirth gathers pace.
We glimpse what we can
From our fearful shelters,
Our own renewal cut off,
Hurried into a strange hibernation,

Our clock is confused,
Our yearly rhythm dislocated.
We should be energised
By pulsating spring.

Instead we are terrorised into half-life,
By a tiny enemy
Which knows no seasons.

Conflagration and Inundation

While Australia burns, we drown,
Having shifted and pulled the world's frame
Out of the shape that held us,
Now turned malignant.

Sufficiency breaks its banks,
Swamping us with our own greed,
A withered and ravaged world catches fire
And consumes us in vengeful flames.

Bur whether we drown or burn,
The Earth is indifferent.
Having survived volcanic fires
And tempestuous primeval storms

It will scarcely register the suicide
Of small creatures who lived on it
For a few brief seconds
Of its history in time and space.

Quiet Spring

Not quite silent
As Carson warned us
Sixty years ago,
But quiet, subdued,
A slow fade out,
Or a long goodbye.

As the volume
Of the morning chorus falls,
Where are the birds?
Flocks of lapwings twisting and turning,
Reduced to three.
Listen hard to hear a curlew or a cuckoo,
A few lonely swifts swoop and screech
Around the house.

Then I read the grim news:
"50% down"; "into the red zone";
"Nearly extinct in Britain".
Something theoretical
Suddenly starkly real.
I remember the hills and dales
Walking carefully to avoid nests,
Dive bombed by snipe
Meadow pipits springing from the ground,
The long, bubbling curlew cry.

She warned us about pollution,
Pesticides, intensive farming.
We barely listened.
Now we have climate change,
Damaging the synchronicity
Between bird and insect.
There is a way back.
Slothed out on consumption,
Do we have the will
To take it?

Swifts

Mid-August and the swifts have gone.
From mid-May they arced across the sky
And screamed with apparent joy.
Now it is quiet and sad without them
Swirling and diving elusively around the house.
They've not honoured me yet with a nest,
And I'm left to contemplate them:
How is your life that is never still?
Wing muscles forever pumping like a non stop heart,
Powering the dancing, swooping flight,
The thousands of miles to hot Africa and back.
You can barely stop to feed your young.
For you, moving must be like breathing:
If you stop, you die.
So you must forever weave your patterns in the air,
Until your wings can move no more,
And you fall to the ground you never knew.

Winter

Bare branches and twigs,
Dancing in the windy, low light
Before a fading pale white sky.
Skies clear, the cold of space
Hardens the ground
Into twinkling frost
And corrugated iron ruts.
Cold grey clouds
Cover the sky from the north.
Snow whirls silently down,
Covering green in white,
Hiding the landscape,
Confusing us, muffling sound.
The cold thaw is slushy wet,
Swelling streams and rivers,
Overflowing muddy banks and fields.

As we wrap our frail bodies,
Evolved nature survives.
A wren, tiny bundle
Of warm feathers,
Flutters among the hedges,
Where a robin stands defiant,
Red breast thrusting into the cold.
Rooks circle, calling in high trees,
Building gravity-defying nests.
The snowdrops heave
Out of the cold ground.

It ends with evening light,
Warmer air, stronger sun
And the colours of spring flowers.

Hannah Silcock

I come from the wild lawless spaces of Northumberland. My family having farmed the same earth on Hadrian's Wall for 300 years.

Having spent an isolated childhood roaming fields, meadows and hills along the banks of the South Tyne River observing livestock and wildlife, I learnt how to listen to them and so understand their lives.

Now through my druid work the ancestors call to me to connect back to the land.

I am inspired by the distant call of the cuckoo, the chatter of migrating geese, the haunting call of the wind as it whistles though a leafless wood, the feel of a butterfly alighting on my hand, the smell of bluebells and the thought that if I am attuned enough, I may see a faerie. The smell of freshly mowed hay and the sight of falling snow, knowing that each snowflake has a different journey, all speak to me. Wow!

The seasons of the year turn, and I turn with them.

The Uncovered Legacy, writing as B.A. Silcock, is my story of the Border Reivers. Available on Amazon.

The Tide Encroaches
Haikus

the sun casts shadows
and as the new tide dallies
it slaps grey flippers

suddenly awake
lines of seals begin to float
off exposed sandbanks

knot, suddenly spooked
lift as one, blot out sunlight
auks and eiders dive

flocks of sandwich terns
pushed by the tide's urgency
all take to the air

when the tide travels
towards us it pushes flocks
of curlews our way

plovers and red shanks
each with different beak lengths
prod the moist shoreline

on the harbour steps
a razorbill sits preening
while herring gulls sleep

lines of dried seaweed
form boundaries on the beach
give warning, DON'T cross

into my pocket
I take handfuls of stones and
ponder their journey

pummeled and battered
and with no audible voice
soon, a grain of sand

Otley Writers & Otley Stanza

Sycamore Gap
23.9.23

there is no answer to why
as the last of my standing people
I had to go, I had to die
for centuries I have guarded this gap
poised and balanced, rooted in purpose
loved and adored by all

I hear your outpouring of grief
as I lie here atop the wall
as my seedlings still hang close
I speak to my companion, Hawthorn,
'I had no choice but to fall your way
yet together our friendship will hold'

but my roots hold fast
my stump remains, I will regrow
for your generations yet to come
and once more I shall watch over
the landscape, our home and see you,
by now ancestors, come and go

but only a small part of me has gone
in this senseless human act
although my heart is torn
and my sadness knows no depths
and our collective souls are ripped
yet, I will not leave you

The Hedge

Earth tremors awoke the Hawthorn.
The dawn chorus halted;
blackbirds' alarm alerted the merle.
Panic set in.
The birds lifted as one.

Clouds of iridescent insects arose,
forming funnels of darkness.
Tree sparrows fled the oncoming destruction.
The injured kestrel, struggling to be free,
still held the half dead vole.

Daffodils covered their ears.
Moles moved new-borns
from crushed tunnels.

Eventually, tractor and flayer stopped.
Nature breathed again.
The littered poisonous spines
awaited bicycle tyres.

The traffic sped past, oblivious.

The Tide Turns

under the cloudless sky
the soul of Scotland
lies across the Solway Firth
awaiting deliverance

the moon has changed her mind
she pulls the ocean away
waves retreat in silence
afraid to land on sandy shore
and nervously wait for those behind
to push them forward once more

a solitary gull flies overhead
a single flap to turn
she smiles at those resting below
with heads gently tucked beneath

flat outcrops lie, layer upon layer
rocks sigh, anticipate another onslaught
its tiny creatures close their eyes
and hide once more in sunken outcrop

a cormorant rides the crest
of white bubbling froth
his feet covered in drifting sea grass,
both uncertain of where to go

he watches shoals of fish,
mouths agape, threatening to absorb
those who venture too close.
'the sea is ours.'

Golden Plover lift as one
sweep across the deserted bedrock
while puffy clouds float gently above
not interested in the chaos below
while long hedges of seaweed
lie still, guarding the shoreline
that liminal space between
land and the unknown

Sandy Wilson

I write novels, memoirs short stories, and occasionally poetry, which I published under my formal Scottish name, Alexander Lothian Wilson.

A retired interior designer I live in Yorkshire with my wife Val, and dog Poppy.

The Caress of Spring appeared in the international poetry anthology Indra's Net, published by Bennison Books.

My own collection of poetry, The Stillness of Certainty is available from Amazon. If you wish you can contact me on sandyajlwilson@gmail.com

Otley Writers & Otley Stanza

Caress of Spring

Spring arrives.
The tantalising
slow caress
of a lover's hand
on my body
as I awake from
deep sleep
dark dreams.

Beautiful Dance of Death

The sun, a pale orb, looks down
as chill winds careen and caper
through the tracery of branches.
Thrumming timeless hymns
Nature's long forgotten songs

Perching on swaying boughs
funereal crows in mourning clothes
flap wings black and feathery.
Trapeze artistes seeking balance
as they cry their discordant chorus

Leaves lose their tenuous grip
Fall, cascading to the ground
to join the multicoloured cavalcade.
Prancing harlequins dancing
across slick grass and damp slab

I stand silent, listen and watch
this wintry, beautiful dance of death

Pond Life

A sleek tern swoops steep
From an overcast sky
Breaking the smooth surface
Into a myriad of mercury droplets
To pluck a shimmering fish
From the pond's dark depths

In a spray of silvery mist
The bird soars, wings beating
Gripped in a sharp red beak
The writhing fish fights for life
Swallowed, it disappears
A magician's conjuring trick

Nearby two swans look away
From this desolate struggle
This death no concern of theirs
They stand sentinel watching
Eight grey cygnets' stumble
Into the mysteries of life

Eternal Clamour

silvery rain gusts past
smoky against a grey sky
and the leaden seething sea

crest of the waves
breaking into spindrift
white flecks of foam

join shrieking gulls
tumbling in tumultuous winds
below in the jagged cleft

of black rocks
indifferent to the incessant
eternal clamour
of the implacable sea

Daily Commute

Worn by the scrape and scuff
Of dragged hobnail boots
The grey cobblestone path
Hemmed by stone walls,
A scar through meadow and copse,
Ends at the dark silhouettes of mills.

Did the workers toiling
Amid the clatter and the stench
Remember.
Remember
The beauty they passed through.
Serenaded by nature's madrigals
In the scent laden morning air.
The heron lifting into the pale blue.
With languid flap of wings.
The shape shifting murmurations.
A squabbling murder of crows
Above the lattice of branches.
The kaleidoscopic feathers
Of the landowner's pheasant.

Or without hope, were they blind
To the beauty they passed through.

Judith Tomlinson

Retired now, having been in teaching for ever, both here in the UK and In Turkiye.

Survived both escapades. Have dabbled in am-dram and enjoyed producing oil pastel and watercolour paintings. Now trying to achieve a long-held ambition .....to write......hopefully......well!

Two Haikus

Silent peace: then dawn floats
Softly over hills painting colour
Onto grey night lines.

Born naked, squalling
Red smeared arms flailing, angry
Greedy at the breast.

Yesterday...Today...Tomorrow

It's wet again
The pouring rain
Seeps out of a sky
So black and grey
The heart sinks;
And soon thinks
Anyone could
Drown in the pools
That flood the roads.

Water overflows the river banks
And no thanks
Are ever given for
The continuous downpour
That cancels summer
At a stroke.
Farmers and people hope
That maybe one day
A ray of sunshine could come their way.

Fond hope, as folk do fight
To have the right
To live...atop the hills
As bodies chilled
Seek out a warm and comfortable spot:
But this is their lot
A summer, wet and dreary too
This much the weather man can do
He smiles and grins at each disaster
Wishing he could be a better forecaster.

Shades

Shades are changing
In thee autumn of our love.
The dazzling gold
Which lightened the springtime
Of our liaison, now turns from gold to brown.

Dull brown, not burnished
To a venerable glow
Full of feeling, inner warmth,
But dull, tarnished, rusted by time,
By lack of care.
Affection absent.

No polish on this old surface
No loving care reflected here.
Just brown, old, crumpled
Brittle and dry, ready to fly,
Away. Like a whisper ready to flutter
Down from the heights.

The tree tops
We soared in with delight,
Lopped low
Down to the dull depths of loneliness.
Winter approaches fast.
Death encroaches.
Only cared for creatures
Survive the cold,
The old, die.
Old love fades to brown
Then grey, colourless, then away,
Soon gone.
Rust, to dust.
Dead.

Pauline Harrowell

I've been a member of Otley Writers for almost twelve years, and still find our meetings stimulating and rewarding.

Poetry and nature are two concepts that always belong to me. I was also the weird little girl with *A Child's Garden of Verse* in one hand, and Ladybird's *British Wild Flowers* in the other. I'm very happy to be part of this project.

Strid Woods

The trees that flamed in autumn
Now smoke in winter
Here, in the river's damp turn
Where sun's rays can't slide through.
Look closer.
Frost beads each twisted twig, stem and stalk
With countless tiny jewels.

This is a place of profusion.
In spring a myriad tiny flies haze the river,
Pointless, yet driven;
Wild garlic crowds the woods
With lush green savoury scents.

Summer floods the valley with tourists,
Chattering, queueing, barbecuing,
Fishing, splashing,
Picnicking, ice-creaming,
Screaming with fun -
Then tired, sticky, happy, home.

Sparrowhawk

She angles through the gap in the hedge.
Brown wings scythe the garden.
The other birds scarper, sharpish;
It was the blackbird nearly bought it.

Frustrated, she perches, cruel queen:
Hungry, lean and mean.
We see her later on the road
Mantling her prey, outraged yellow eyes
Outglaring the car's headlights,
Defying us to take the ex-pigeon.

Why do I take her part?
The pigeon too is a marvel,
Hardwired for navigation and speed,
Its plumage gleams more varied than the hawk's.
Yet grace with ferocity wins every time.

Summer 2013

After a summer that never was,
Spring was freakishly late;
The saturated land force-fed with rain,
Blind bulbs stabbed up through soggy soil
Blasted by swirls of icy snow;
A pair of waxwings are blown off track,
Exotic, desperate for home.

The grass won't grow in the mud fields;
The sodden crops won't germinate
And lambs are born misshapen.

Far away the parched land gasps for water,
Bones the only crop it grows.

Being a Bittern

I am the essence of leaning,
one with wind and rushes.
Russet streaks my breast.
I glare, alien yellow eye.

Stalky legs straddle stalks.
I skulk. I swing in swamps,
reach through wind-rustling reeds,
stab my bill at the sky.

I am rare. They yearn for me,
to tick me off their list.
It pleases me to tease
so I crank out my cry.

Did I mention booming?
I fill my tawny throat,
Throb and throw my voice:
Once bittern, always shy.

Questions from a two year old

The see-saw stops. A thought clouds her bright clear face.
"Don't want the leaves come down. Put them back."
I explain the passage of the seasons,
The trees' ritual sacrifice a promise of next year's growth.

"Where do the leaves go?"
The worms eat them, I say, turn them into new soil
So the trees will grow stronger,
Then birds will eat the worms.

Now we are at the millpond.
Mobbed by ducks, greed on webbed feet.
"Could a duck eat me?"
And now I try not to think of Ilkley Moor...

Pam Line

Life is full of weird and wonderful stories and a lot of them seem to happen to me. Every day a page turns to reveal life at its quirkiest. Chance encounters, happy events, and tragedy mix in a mélange of experiences. In my writing, I try to capture the nub of what has happened possibly somewhat exaggerated.

My collection of short stories True Lies and memoir Line Dancing are available from Amazon.

Endlessly Beautiful

To hear the birds chirrup and coo,
To watch them collect twigs,
To imagine eggs,
To foresee squawking chicks.
To be in Kettlewell at dawn.
To hear the clip clop of hooves,
To feel the goosebumps as they cross
The bridge
To the smithy.
To feel the anticipation.
To don the socks and boots,
To walk towards the unknown.
To see the carpet,
To melt at the view,
To smell the wood,
To capture the sight
To experience the sylvan swathe
To be privileged to see
To thrill
To the sight of bluebells.
To marvel that
To me, from today, a sight indelible,
To be forever in my memory.

Thornwick Bay

Hush no-one knows I'm here
On the beach listening to the hiss
Of pebbles swooshing up
Swooshing down filling pools
With a swish of water, green algae
Waving tendrils to welcome
Crabs looking for shelter from
The crunchy rock-strewn shore.
I put some in my candy-striped
Bucket to give them breathing space.
Chalk cliffs gleam and glitter
Busy with squiggly dots wheeling
Gulls circling screeching landing
And taking off again to defend their
Territory, my territory.
Cutlass between my teeth scanning
The cliffs for marauders.
Hist, faded voices. I leap from one giant
Boulder to another crossing chasms
Towards the cave. Unseen bony
Fingers reaching up to grab my bare
Feet to drag me down into the deep.
Hush, listen. 'Hold her steady.' 'Aye
Aye, Captain.' The gentle plash of oars
Stroking, caressing, quieting a merciless
North Sea until my breathing is
The only echoing sound to be heard
In the dark cavern. Clang clang
The lunch bell sounds as I run
Up through carpets of primroses
Towards the cottage for food stomach
Rumbling, past the pillbox,
Up and up till broaching the top
Grandmother stands smiling as I show
Her my crabs scrambling over one another
Wondering where the sea has gone.

Top to Bottom.

Noon in England, two pm in Greece
[Mad dogs and Englishmen go
Out in the noonday sun.]
Mediterranean sky outlining
The monastery on the ridge, a vertical hike
For the brave in the not-so-cool
Of a morning in Kalymnos.
[Some young Danes did it this morning.]
Below rock-strewn terrain devoid of trees
Until halfway down scrubby pines
Cling at strange angles pondering
When they can fall over and relax.
Rows of square houses like childish
Drawings. Three windows, terrace, door
Underneath in the middle.
A cantilever-roofed house pops up
Giving shade to pigeons before they swoop
Down to drink from the hotel pool.
Earlier it was the turn of the house martins,
Skimming the water, lifting off with the
Reflection of blue on their bellies. Through the
Plastic railings of the balcony outside our room.
I can see four young people cavorting in the
Pool. Years drop away as I remember. The girls
Have buds for breasts covered with scanty
Triangles of fabric tied at the back and around
The neck with narrow straps for the sake
Of modesty. The boys alec about, try to duck the girls,
Catch them around the ankles and pull them under the
Water. Screams and giggles follow.
Oh, to be young again.

Roland Cam

'Everybody has something of value to say – even if it's a surprise! We just need to learn to listen, better.'

The whole point of writing is to entertain and if you find something to enjoy in some of my poetry - at least for some of the time, then that's a start.

I have three books close to publication. Hell Hides in many Hollows, The Cult of the Dead and Sorceress of All Rome. A fourth book, The Pact of the Troika is a work in progress.

The Geese are Always First

I watch for the signs.

The geese are always first
                    that I notice
                    Heading West-Northwest in loose Arrowhead
                                              Formation
                          Fast moving silhouettes
                              against a stark,
                        dry, grey sky
          While the other birds cluster and chatter
Then the boss peck stills them

Black Crows begin to gather and muster
              joining passing black flights in one great movement
              Heading North-West-North
        quickly, in the late October Sun

I begin tidying away in the garden.
While the more 'hardy' gather food.

The 'Canary's' come warmly into mind.

Nocturnal Visitor

It triggered the lights
then loitered
lit up - for everyone to see
it tip-toed around the plant pots
not a scurry – as a rat
but cute
nimble
with dignity
like a small dog, sniffing
I'd keep and learn to know it
A cute, little pig living quietly in my hedge

Jaques Cousteau
For One Incredible Day

They called it a 'Pig Ray,'
– a Manta for sure,
the size of the thing
– just left me in awe,
I swam on my back,
while it blocked out the Sun,
It swam overhead,
Just inches above.
to see such as this!
how lucky am I?

a little time later,
in midst of shoal,
a large flash of silver,
Barracuda!
with ragged jaws of teeth like a frightening saw,
flashed right and left,
then left
in hunt of something more bite-size
Now on the ledge
look over the ridge
Tiger Shark basking
– a shark by a cliff!
We didn't stay long
I took out my mouthpiece
to share
my oxygen bubbles

with an Angel Fish who gulped at them in the most joyful way
Just for a day, I was Jacques Cousteau
And it was unforgettable

Ron Millet

Words were a daily part of my livelihood as a printer and also as a local politician. As I grew older and with a visit to Auschwitz over a decade ago both revealed the inadequacy of prose in describing one's emotional reactions to extreme situations.

Then I re-discovered poetry. By saying less directly but more by implication and oblique imagery, a deeper picture is painted. More than 100 poems later I still think of writing poetry as an act of daring and bravery - the emotional equivalent of hang gliding.

North Yorkshire

Litton and Wharfe, Malham and Swale;
limestone lips on grass layered heights.
Low whispered welcomes from hill and from dale.
Not chapel lush from the South Wales valleys
nor prim, proper, patchwork
of stockbroker England.
Rather, rough rocks set in green grandeur
by lone farms founded in bleak beauty
from bright lime shades to sky touching purple
in landscape sweeps of fields, forest and moor

A still sound of deep breath, driving
slight sighs to shrug off scents of the city.
Rare sun glazing days of summer
piercing the corners of every bright shade.
Perfect scenes under a sublime sky;
a few fluffed up clouds scattered above
rock strewn streams, butterfly browsed, threaded through
dry stone walls built in tidy disorder.
We who visit here, paroled and allowed,
curated by sheep, avoiding the crowd.

A Promise

There's a soft edge to Winter's knife
easing its drawn out daily cut.
Fresh slight scents, frozen until now,
hint at new grass, warm paving stones,
shouting songbirds and flushed bare skin:
all bathing in the comforting sun.

But not quite yet....

Fragile wands of green bunched together
suggesting, soon to be, daffodils
cannot magic the spurned chill away.
First the restless sky must have her say.
A farewell for the surplus lover
that travels on blustery winds each night
bringing his frost of false purity.

Each day the bright sky delays the leaving,
edging the horizon a little more
with melting shades of red then pink then grey,
to return in the morning, summoned by
a noisy indignation of birdsong.
Thinking of the dawning's awkward recall
the pinks and reds grow stronger towards night
taking longer to fade, as if to say,

It's almost 'Goodbye' -

Away from here but not quite gone:
dismal days still need a cleaning.
We promise to bring your old friend,
the new Spring, with us tomorrow,
maybe next week if she can come...

Or sometime soon...

Swift

Humid heat from the season's sleepy haze;
unfolding flowers for their ritual rape
by vagrant wasps and bees that bumble by
while wisps of gnats and flies, midges and mites
hourly itch our rash of irritation ;
held at bay by occasional dusk time bats
and the daily swing of summer swallows
free trapezing through their skin itching prey.

Then comes the Swift, scimitar smooth
elegant and easy; sweeping,
soaring over street, park and field
Pack chattering through alleyways.
A tail twitch and turn, quick-stepping
past the pale pedestrian pace
of a slow moving House Martin.
Air cleaning, exciting the eye;
an intimation of angels,
The effortless prince of the skies.

Bramble

Walking the Autumn day's declining way
inside a fret of thorn protected branchings
bright, black boot polished, beaded berries hide.
Simpering silent smirks from under lowered leaves
with modest glances at our hungry eyes.
'Come close and sample me.'
Not the mono taste of ripened strawberries
whimpering for their clotted cream.
Nor the electric rip of ripe redcurrants
charioteering across the tongue.
But the gritty bunching of bramble tastings
always changing from fruit to fruit.
The sour sharp rebuke of being wrenched too soon.
A full sweetness when the time is right.
Last, the late pick of comfort in a mouthful:
rich, overblown, autumnal unction.
Waning warmth and an ochre wooded wasteland
shadowed by the, soon to be, winter sun.
A moment of childhood recalled for free
from the edges and untended hedges
as gratitude for being left untouched.

Mark Robinson

I write poetry about a fragile planet where every life form is connected. For this anthology I have focused on the threatened land environment, on challenges facing people and the life forms people depend on, and on mysteries of the earth. As always, I try to look outwards with a personal response.

    Being part of Otley Writers is a great and varied experience with newer and older members, and it is the fellowship that still motivates me to keep writing.

Tarn

Unexceptional
Old strollers
Anglers patient for a carp
Canada geese, mallards, tufted ducks,
Kids licking Yorkshire ice-creams
A woman with rollator persists, a full circuit.
Coots nesting in reeds
A couple feed knowing cygnets
Volunteers clearing algae
Cormorants hang out proudly in a row
Small sailboats wave offshore
Drifts of an ordinary sky
Mums in hijabs picnic
With their kids under a sheltering oak
Fewer butterflies, the third hottest day the world has ever seen
In a row……no dragonflies yet
Though as the nearby plane trails off, it's passing mild.
Great crested preening,
Swallows curling, looping, bending restless,
Hybrid ducks are blending
'Hello', a girl in a body brace calls to us all
'Hello'- this life in unassuming place is special.
Tendrils floating, legs in motion,
Flavours of release, savouring peace
Eyes greet, a splash of commons
'Hello' half-strangers cry - space here for all.

Otley Writers & Otley Stanza

Study the Wings

She studies the wings of the dead
Blue tit before arranging a burial
She holds it high, as if to fly
Her focus is the colours, filaments, thread

Of survival, petal veins
On wings, brushed feathers, broom
Tail. Her gaze is intense
She explores what a predator disdains

She cares for connection, fingers
Restore the bird to flight
Arms outstretched to pale sky
Eyes invoke spirit that lingers.

This is not an autopsy, her outcry
Against disposable waste culture
Starts early, she reveres
Each flutter in a cold breeze, asks why

Some birds no longer fly, her eyes
Are not yet veiled, she is five
Her mind is not barred from
Being wise, she will scrutinize

The fragile prize and try to understand
Before the spade turns the soil.
Young arms reach to immense sky
Gentlest touch extends the bird's span.

From a photograph: Tilda with Dead Blue tit   By Danny Burrows

Polar Bear

Franz Joseph Land's archipelago thaws
And glacial mountains drip away.
An apex predator slumps on a shrunk
Fragment of his ancient hunting ground.

Fridtjof Nansen Land, once, then seized
By Russians for military purposes.
What's in a name? Caribou vanished here
2000 years ago - climate changed.

The polar bear's fur is stain-brown
And white. Maybe he can't figure
How to adapt; if dark now thrives.
Mirroring melt-light, his compass is lost,

Breath holes have all shifted.
A failed, three-day swim for seals
Strands him unseasonably far
From snacks - snow geese, crowberries.

His tail hangs in slush water.
A genetically suited mate might be just
A distant sliver, drifting nowhere fast.
Keystone species are disconnected.

Paws are folded under his chin,
Gaze shrinks into a somnolent
Sink of evolutionary murk.
Thaw contracts his sombre girth.

Locked down, without protection
Or delivery service. Caged, with no kind
Scientific keeper. *Nanook, Oshkúj, Umka, Isbjørn* ...
Trapped in the hunger games of *Anthropocene*.

And rain falls on the *Greenland* ice sheet.
And rainbow children's 'weave back' street haikus
Show resolve-melting dollar bills
A true north - of countless tipping points.

Otley Writers & Otley Stanza

OTLEY STANZA

We are poetry group based in Otley and draw members from elsewhere in West Yorkshire and beyond. We're affiliated to The Poetry Society.
An active and friendly group of poets we meet online every Wednesday and monthly on Sundays. 'In person' meetings are held on occasional Sundays at the Courthouse.

Find out more at https://poetrykeeps

Terry O'Connor

A worn-out academic, Terry O'Connor lives in Burley-in-Wharfedale, where he reads, writes, gardens and talks to the neighbours' cats. He likes classical music, wild places and birdsong, dislikes hypocrisy and celery, and cooks a mean shepherd's pie. Like most retired men, he is generally to be found on his allotment or asleep.

Limpet

A byword for attachment,
rock-bound, robust, thick-shelled,
hard to shift when clamped down
in the one safe place,
all softness hidden, no way in.

Feeding cautiously, locally,
systematically strimming algae
from nearby rocks, side to side,
slowly forward, safety first,
graze, hide, every tide the same.

You should get out more, limpet.
Other rocks, different algae,
whole new cliffs and harbour walls,
a world of novelty, of difference.
Or is it that from which you hide?

Nuthatch, Treecreeper

They pass in silence,
no pause or sideways glance,
almost palpable nonchalance.

One heads downwards,
bright in blue-grey and peach,
belligerently brash.

One hop-scrabbles upwards,
drab brown, pale-flanked,
resolute, focussed.

One loudly confident,
one quietly discreet,
each disregards the other.

A metaphor, perhaps?
On life's busy tree-trunk
just be yourself.

Otley Writers & Otley Stanza

Overnight Guests

While I slept, an Old Lady dropped by
attended by several Common Footmen,
sleek in their grey and golden livery,
and by a stout, white-dusted Miller.

Welcome visitors all, enticed by light
to the dark heart of a glowing cube
that promised a place of sanctuary
through the cooling hours before dawn.

Uncover the moth trap gently.
Lift out egg-boxes one by one,
inspect their folds and cavities
for Bird-Cherry Ermine and Mother of Pearl.

Green Carpets fly off in agitation,
Yellow Underwings withdraw to their hollows.
The Old Lady has made herself comfortable
and is in no hurry to be moved.

There is a point, of course, in catching moths.
Identifying, counting – it's citizen science.
But also the simple courtesy of greeting those
who came visiting while I slept.

David Cattanach

On moving to Otley engaged in extra-mural creative writing courses at Swarthmore Centre, Leeds. In addition, studying screen writing and a study of leading authors such as D H Lawrence, Sylvia Plath and Joseph Conrad. David has enjoyed preparing work for Otley Writers, Otley Poets and had work published in various 'online' journals.

Beech Trees

I brought her ashes
across the Village Green, through the garlanded field gate,
to the foot of the majestic trunk.
Outstretched hands spread a fine dust
of her among trees which once held a view.
Her rooms marked years of occupation,
often filled with recorded female voices.
Years of medical training warned of fatal outcome
but she still offered Samaritan smile to failing lives.
I wanted her face to talk of seasons
And be able to count with her the falling leaves.
We siblings mutter soft words now.
Breezes disturb, beetles forage, jet trails score the sky.
Then I listen for her dust rubbing the beeches' frame.

Towards Spring

Standing in the wood where anemones grow,
Here hibernating timber waits among the toppled ones.
Webs gossamer floats, shimmering between the silver birch.
It is an end to March, of greenness getting greener,
Soon fountains of swallows flight will ignite
The horizon line.
I walk now among the black obelisks
Raising my head, feeling the creak of neck bones,
To hear the sighing of branches touching.
Buds burst, blossom breaks dropping seed, spreading scents,
A smell of honey pollen drenches the air.
Knots and knarls call time on the banked earth.
Many children are born on this day,
Breaking through mothering sacks.
Leaf bursts on me and I hear the infant cry.

Ripple

It's an overcast day,
ten chimney pots sit unmoving
in a river reflection.
Above, are seabirds and feral pigeons
snaking, changing form,
weave over surface ripples.
Inspiration, ideas, sit in the troughs
flying, just as high as those forms
that twist and bend.
Even though the chimney pots
remain fixed and at attention!!

Summer

The numb beast of winter has vanished,
Replaced by song from sky and hedgerow.
Scents run on the updraft – hay is cut.
Thunderbugs spot forearms coated in sweat.

Meadows lay unshorn, tall,
Seedheads of long grasses
Filter through the haze,
Like so many longbows into the blue.

Beneath the oak and the spiny thorn
Cattle rest – in a shady place.
Image, caught as forever,
Seized, and placed in a Corot painting.

Walking this landscape
Little things jolt the mind,
Broken stile there, a whiplash of bramble there,
Wool torn from sheep, or a crow atop a gate.

Summer lazy, animals in collapse,
Bees lick a moist ditch,
Hollyhocks trumpets sing
To bare stone walls.

The mind seems to stretch
Into the forever.
Ideas fly, to work on distant
Horizons, even those that are hidden.

Hotel La Deu

Perched upon a fragment of land.
Nearby, pool of spring water rises at a crossroads.
Damselflies dance among the reeds;
Beads of dew encircle strands.
Mother collects water in plastic bottles
To be used in part for Hector's evening bath.
Shepherded sheep flock at adjacent crossroads,
Noses cresting ground, smelling,
A namesake, black Gilliflower Apple
Offers thick, tasty puree, also known as Sheep's Nose.
Painters try to set down
With hands a sublime composition.
In its low slung depression
The spring pool shimmers.
Hotel La Deu presents
Patatas de la Deu,
Famed in La Garrotza.
I consume wine that shines, as water
Runs through another's fingertips.

Barry Cowperthwaite

Poetry is my way of exploring selfhood, and my ideas largely develop from feelings and memories stirred up in response to elements of nature and the landscape. I have had poems published online and in arts festival pamphlets and can sometimes find the courage to perform them.

Blue tit

You bustle about
without pretension
intent only on
hungry bellies
back home

unaware of or
indifferent to
the bright allure of
your jacket of blue
and the yellow vest

making your business
purely practical
you tolerate my slow
advance towards the
feeder then you're off

pebble from a
catapult winging
into the dark mesh
smaller by the yard
until you vanish

Buddleia

Pointing your own path
yearning virile arrowing
into the blue blushing with
anticipation and here they come
alighting white crimson black
unwitting little propagators
of your lofty purpose.

Goldfinch

Strutting dandy
annoyingly aware of just
how good you look
next to the sparrows you
bully off the feeder. Hah!
How does it feel to be
ousted by that
bullfinch?

Here comes your
gang down from the wire
to claim the perches as if you all
owned the place, and for a while
you do, humbling the dunnocks
as they peck crumbs
fallen from your lofty
realm.

But I see
the hanging hatchet
of a kestrel, circling
discreet as an executioner
and you may well find
that your gaudy opulence
could prove to be
your downfall.

Heron

Your hate-etched eye had already seen me;
huffed out of deep time you beat away,
oozing resentment. I see you
settle upstream, refusing me
even a glance, sulked
into the slow current,
stabbing, indignant.

It means nothing to you
that I think you beautiful
as a Giacometti, elemental,
stripped of all but necessity,
pure pointed intent. You fling me
one belligerent, tortured vowel then
you are gone, leaving me wondering.

Jo Peters

Jo Peters has been successful in competitions and has been published in magazines. Her pamphlet 'Play' was published by Otley Word Feast Press and her collection 'like yellow, like flying' by Half Moon Books. She has recently completed a series of poems about the woman known as St Hilda of Whitby.

Sparrowhawk

I open my kitchen door
to your outraged stare just a yard away.

I didn't know your legs were so long, so yellow,
standing there on my garden table,
your claws so sharp, your beak so curved.

I'd heard the soft thud on my window,
but am not prepared for the fury of your yellow eyes.
I feel the need to apologise for the inconvenience,
the presence of my house, the glass trick.

Sudden lift-off, quick wing-beats leave a hole
in the air, a feathery smudge on my window,
in my head.

Not Just Words

Written on reading that many words referring to the natural world have been removed from the latest edition of the Oxford Junior Dictionary

Was there a committee in charge of de-naturing,
of displacing, disconnecting, unseasoning?
Whichever sharp-suited young employee of OUP,
deputed to de-clutter, de-flower from A to E,
scythed a swathe of bluebells and buttercups,
sprayed all the dandelions and the cowslips.
Was it you who deleted adder and acorn,
who cancelled conker (conker!) cygnet and catkin?

Say acorn, you have the curve of a light brown nut,
miniature egg, snug in rough-to-touch cup,
a pixie pipe. You have shades of Autumn woods
where jays squawk and squirrels hide winter food.
You have ancient oaks, seasoned beams for a house,
a solid family table, pannage, the Mary Rose.

Night Shift

Had I not been so tired I'd have missed you,
but I went to bed early in the June dusk
when you were just setting about your business.

A bird with a face gliding low over meadow grasses;
a white shadow, quartering the field, listening.
From my window I felt the spell of your industry.

You came and you went so unexpectedly,
now black against a fading sky, wings
stark triangles, something small in your talons.

The Dunnock Chicks

curl in blue shells,
grow, spear through
thin prison walls
to find a larger world,
safe, softly round,
in which to be blind,
naked, gaping for food.

At sundown, tired,
how gently and warmly
the grey-brown bird
settles and broods.

The chicks' eyes open.
Through the stark
prickly criss- cross
of hawthorn twigs,
see fragments
of immeasurable blue.

Scraps of shell
lie hidden in grass below,
pieces of the sky that fell.

Kevin Holloway

Kevin Holloway is a poet and writer based in Bradford, West Yorkshire. He enjoys exploring and understanding place, and the interaction with place of individuals and communities over time. His first pamphlet, Out of Place, from which the three poems here are taken, was published by Half Moon Books in 2019. His work has been included in the Leeds based poetry journal Strix, and included in anthologies.

Salmon

I walked beside wide fast water,
in a low place where provision
is received when given
not sought and caught by human will.

I was far down in reverie
when a salmon leapt three men high,
hung while the world and I
moved still and silent under it.

The salmon's arc of fall was clear;
I held out my arms as river
and thrilling living silver
landed stagger-heavy in them.

I pulled the fish against my chest;
as long as a man's striding tread
and deeper than his head,
all over, brief rainbows dripping.

I knelt, its weight across my thighs,
gills failing in the too thin air,
the golden round-eyed stare
an invitation beckoning.

I wasn't wise enough to know
the wisdom I was being shown,
I let the salmon down,
down in the quick river's running.

Otley Writers & Otley Stanza

Stepping Stones

Where it's wide, stepping stones cross the river.
Thirty-eight, but none cared for; some sinking,
others sliding, I doubt I'd get over
now without wet feet or a full soaking.
I crossed them once, years ago; went with care,
watching each footstep land, but fast, driven
by some sense I'd topple in if I dare
slow down and lose my forward motion.

But on the centre stone I stopped, turned upstream;
a great plain of mirrored autumn colour,
vast to my smallness, was coming downstream
towards me. The delight of something never
seen before caught me, and standing out there,
so exposed, I felt a thrill of small fear.

Debris

The river's dropped its level overnight
and like an ebbing tide left a washed-flat
arc of beach, but tiny, a cliff-backed
cove in miniature, a childhood's delight.
Look, bobbing in towards the beach a small
red speed-boat crewed by a rat and hamster.
Oh! Wasp-waisted Barbie's on her lounger,
Ken's stiff-limbed climbing up the sheer cliff wall.

Debris of all sorts on these little beaches,
sticks, leaves, bits of rope, tangled on the shore.
And oddments that I recognise too well:
the rorschach of the river catches
debris of my own, stuff I might ignore
when it's half-submerged and hidden by the swell.

Dave Barthram

My poetry is inspired by the place of my birth, Malhamdale. Its rolling hills, the meandering river Aire and fifty years walking the Pennine Way surveying birds for the BTO have brought me joy and happiness and an increased awareness of the power of nature.

Otley Writers & Otley Stanza

Aerial Accident

Two carrion crows
        quarter the beach
                              searching for
                              food.

Two oystercatchers,
        like spitfires in a dog fight,
frantically buzz them,

until they collide,
fall out of the sky
and hit the sand.

They lie unmoving until,
disturbed by my approach,
one takes off.

The other lies on its back,
wings trapped under its body,
and watches.

I pick it up carefully,
turn it to unwind its neck
and set it down.

Immediately
    it flies off
                      to rejoin
                          its mate.

Death in the Aire

In
the
tree tops
chattering
starlings
suddenly
fall silent
and
fly away
as a female
sparrow hawk
clutching one
in her talons
circles down
to the river
below
to hold
it under
the water
until satisfied
her prey is dead

Barn Owl

The pale, heart shaped face
quartering the field margin
on gold spangled wings,
almost stalls as it flies
slowly and silently
alongside the
hawthorn
hedge,
head
down,
listening
for tell tale
noises in the
rough grass.

A field vole
foraging for food,
underneath the
dying stems
suddenly
feels talons
in his back….

Three owlets
in their nest
welcome
the arrival
of supper.

Two Weasels

totally absorbed
in combat
tumbling over
each other
fight their
way along
the snow
covered path
glistening with
morning frost
pay me
no attention
as they
roll between
my feet
continue into
the distance
and out
of sight

Sandra Burnett

Sandra Burnett is an Otley Poet and enjoys reading and writing poetry. Her pamphlet New Lease and collection Between sea and sky were published by Half Moon Books.

Dandelion

Hey Dandy – aren't you the cheeky one
snuggled in bed with those hybrids.

It's a puzzle where you get your looks
when, as a bud, you're not promising
and eagerly embrace the punk craze
with your spikey head.

but look at you today, flashy as the sun,
tap root anchored.

I've seen your brothers on the lawn,
laying low with pink-tipped daisies,
and your cousins on the riverbank
under the blackberry's bush

sniffing garlic, dreaming of brew-ups
with burdock.

and all of you addicted to the bees;
need to honey them over and over
until you go seedy, grow weedy,
like some stubbed cigarette

Gathered round the oak, frail elders wait,
and here's the rub –

Your sort breeze along on a child's puff.

Pipistrelle

I'm one of those common Pipistrelle bats
that roost in the Church of St. John.
And I heard the vicar complain to his wife
repairs can't be done 'till we've gone.

But our nursery colony has been set up
after winter's enforced hibernation.
I can't, for a moment, see us moving on,
even though he's bought loft insulation.

How soon he's forgotten how we all turned up
on the night of the Scouts' barbeque,
and swallowed the gnats and midges that bite.
We don't get the credit we're due.

So, we've folded our wings, and tightened our toes,
and hang from the oak beamed trapeze,
regularly dropping our bodily waste,
an act we perform with great ease.

And I should be happy, in such a fine home,
with the trees by the pond now long gone,
'cos I'm only a common Pipistrelle bat
that roosts in the Church of St. John.

Gail Mosley

Gail Mosley lives in Leeds and is a long-standing member of Otley Stanza. She has read at Chapel FM and appeared in various anthologies. All kinds of observation or childhood memories can spark a poem.

Only Birds
(On the backway from Brockweir)

We pull up sharp.
A rugby ball of streaked plumage stands,
thin legs rooted to the camber of the road.
It's unmoved by our hoot.
I get out and approach. It stands.
I shoo. It stares with ice-black eyes.
No choice, I close my hands around its warmth;
a quiver of heart resonates
down long quills. I half place, half throw
it into long grass under the hedge,
safer, for a while.

Further on two full-grown buzzards in a field
peck for worms.
Your child is grounded up the road,
I want to call.
And these are only birds.

Otley Writers & Otley Stanza

Animate

I'm surprised people don't climb into my arms more often.
This one strokes my bark, peels a soft flake free,
I don't mind,
settles on an outstretched limb
rests one foot in a cleft
stays safe from the midday sun.

We are a close-knit group, mulberry, holly and me.
Our mingled canopy hangs low to shelter
birds and animals
and such a one as this
who comes to sit a while
breathing the air we breathe.

At Menai Bridge

Under a new moon beside the Strait,
in this basin lined with dusky reeds
between the thorn bush
where a blackbird sings the sunset down
and the water's edge
a heron stands and stretches its neck.

Pilferer

Weren't the fallers good enough?
You had to skitter up to the top of the tree
where the biggest, rosiest, apples grew,
pick your own, jaw clenched round it
leap-frog down,
make off into another garden
not just once - when I looked again
most of the crop had gone.

You even cached one in a flower tub,
swapped it for a tulip bulb.

Well you've done it now
squirrel

Bruce Barnes

Bruce Barnes is a Bradford based poet but an offcomedun from London. He's a member of Otley Stanza, and his poems have appeared in Pennine Platform, Strix, and London Grip. He's a past winner of the Ilkley Literature Festival Poetry Prize. His pamphlet *Isreal – Palestine* was published by Otley Word Feast in 2016.

The Roost

I watch dark gather around the covers,
growing lighter where it meets the white
of your ruffled hair. You call from a dream,
I don't know what, but it seems to echo
the jackdaws of days ago-

having heard their clatter in the valley near us,
you took a grove as their gathering place;
thereafter, evenings were you mud scrambling
to another vantage point, scanning the twilight
for their roost. I went along with it,
sticking to a drier path, snatching at the glitter
of ornithology imparted: smaller than rooks,
the youngsters with duller plumage, and how
they mate for life. Once we watched the twist
and tumble of a 'train', not the stuff of starlings
but still brief and glorious before they flew
across the city ; back home, you laughed
as I speculated their roost from a map

-towards morning, your cries are over,
and as light returns, I watch you as you are.

The Holly Tree

We risk lightning strikes and bad hair days
from witches, by cutting the holly back;
looking beyond superstition,
I notice the tree's roughly pruned hand-grenade
shape that takes far too much light.
I give Rob encouragement, a bowsaw,
loppers, and shears; he is the provider
of muscle and some measured determination.
(We go back a long way, fifty years
to a Leeds terraced house, holly-bare at Christmas.)
He starts at the outer branches and burrowing towards the trunk,
berry-less most years but shelter for birds.
Gathering the wands of spiny masculine
I sense through heavy gloves their ugly thorns
scratching palms and at my conscience. I want Rob
to rest, stay the bowsaw's to and fro,
and if there is time, let the ambiguity
of consequences bite with the blades' teeth,
a contained row of steely witches' hats.

Otley Writers & Otley Stanza

Tête-à-têtes

Thanks for including me
in your private conversation, but no need,
your bellied, petalled talk, like a town crier's,
bellows through the first day of Spring, broadcasting
to receptive yellow stoned back to backs,
and the preoccupied
by sky. A slick of ivy
your feet colours the message somewhat-
yellow are the gardeners who dare not climb
the shed to mend your cracked pot,
yellow again is the warning of danger,
until it daubs a flag on the ship of fools.
A wind wags your masts, your thin stems:
there's a conversation to be had
on that jaundiced subject, with no answer
to the question 'So what do we do now?'

Big Garden Bird Watch

I was one for bean counting, before my look-out
stint from the porch; glass played there with a plenty
of reflected heads craning and me doing what I shouldn't-
adding the wheeling of gulls and their proper gliding.
(It's not really flying over). I shift my perch
flex the back, and return to the ground rules,
to a dunnock, just the one scratting about beneath
the bay bush. Once there was a ménage à trois,
bickering and taking off in a huff but not now:
10am-ish, overcast and the light unashamed
above the velux, a wind flexing the roosting tree.
Any other time, I would be counting the same world twice.

The End

Printed in Great Britain
by Amazon